G000138889

Levée

A Poetry Cookbook

Levée

A Poetry Cookbook

Consuelo and Guy Barker

GILGAMESH
PUBLISHING LTD

Levée

Published by Gilgamesh Publishing in 2017
Email: info@gilgamesh-publishing.co.uk
www.gilgamesh-publishing.co.uk
ISBN 978-1-908-53192-9
© Consuelo Barker 2016

Acknowledgements

Terry McCormick for your photography, Emily Hudson for your help with typing and filing Guy's work, Phoebe Ray for helping to arrange, Elspeth Sinclair for editing and proofing, Tom Waugh for the beautiful stone you carved for Guy and Dorothee Giedroyć for your photographs of his headstone.

And thank you, Thabo Lemisola for your brilliant nursing care. Guy wished so much for you and your family.

CIP Data: A catalogue for this book is available from the British Library

For our two children, Theodora and Inigo

INTRODUCTION

For this book, I have combined the poetry and thoughts of my late husband, Guy Barker, with photographs of dishes and recipes. Our shared enjoyment of cooking, eating and entertainment was a pivot around which our family moved and my wish is to breathe new life into his work through what we loved doing most. In putting this book together, I have wanted to recapture some of the person we have lost.

Guy wrote all his life. He worked as a stockbroker to support his family but his passion had been for poetry. Born in 1960, he died in 2009 from cancer, after a long fight.

One volume of his poems in 2006 caught the imagination of the then poet laureate, Ted Hughes. I have included this letter at the back.

My book begins with photographs that depict Guy's early life as suggested to me in his poems. I imagine him in a comfortable nest and then tipped out into new and alien surroundings 'of unfathomable darkness.'

The photographs track his poetry across water, land and wood towards a clearing.

I have used food and its preparation as an accompaniment to the poems to look at their flavour and meaning.

Some of these dishes are entirely mine and others have been adapted.

Ingredients I cook and style with are:

    Samphire to mean SEA,

    Bull rush to mean BIRTH,

    Flat bread to mean EXILE,

    Fish to mean THE EXPLORER,

    Salt to mean TEARS,

    Onions to mean IDENTITY,

    Leaves to mean OFFERING,

    Herbs to suggest different types of taste so sour, sweet, bitter or mordant,

    Flowers to mean LUSCIOUS,

    Wire to mean UNFOLDING,

    Spices to mean SWADDLING,

    Fire to mean UNION,

    Yokes of egg to mean RENEWAL,

    I use black to denote the subconscious mind and bright colours for manifestation.

    SEPIA is for memory.

My future as a poet

Chapters

O C E

A N S

'To sit in one's own fantastic expression, to delve with straining hands to the space below your mind, before your existence, to ask. IF I am not a drop of something quite sui generis, if I am from a womb that was not mine, a body that was fashioned by yet another body before that one, and so on, what am I? Have I claims to be found within myself in this hour, or must I turn back, look to the stem, to the branch, to the trunk and, and so to the roots? And if I am of another, am I to make with my seed a greater Tree, or am I to grow, bloom, and wither and be forgotten? To do all this, must be important.'

Must I remain here?

Or should I throw myself out?

To Sea

OVER

LAND

'water wet in

my closed eye...'

BREAKING WEBS

1978

Standing ferocious and futile on the South's Head's

Wonderful cliff, mother

Said she dreamt that one of us, dead,

Before her little eyes,

Told that water drowns and bodies, fed

With the universe of fish

Rise up, and beckon, and with rounded,

Worn-over bones, rattle

A song that sounds terrifying, wild.

So, I thought, moral

Is, never ever be born and stay a child.

And that is why I offered,

Murmuring, my mouth full, my words mild,

To the other members,

The gang who gave me laws, life, who filed

Me down to Yes and No,

OR, perhaps, one day, when I have grown.

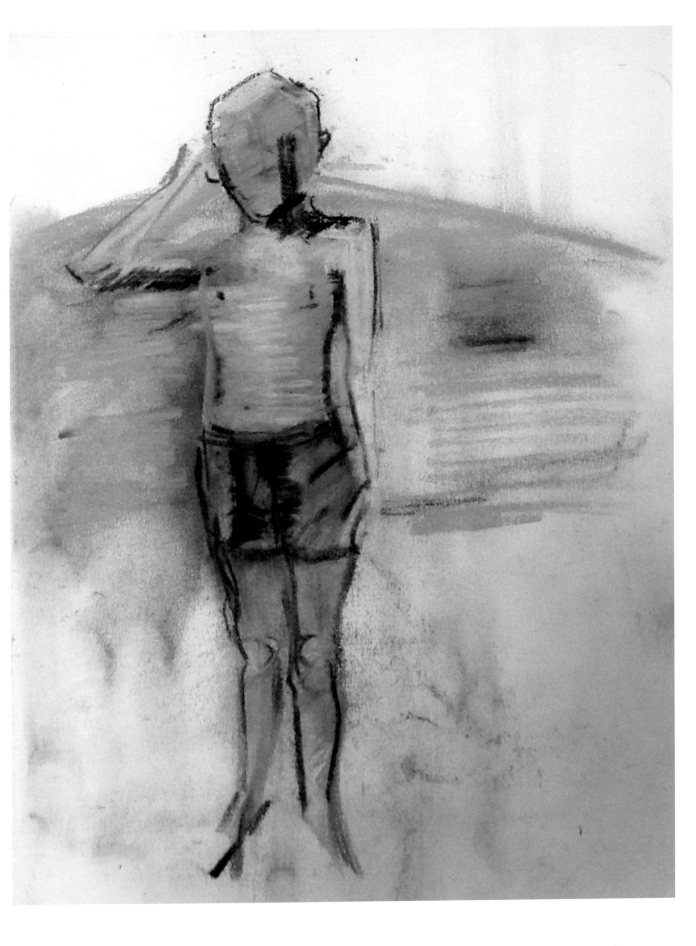

BLACK INK RISOTTO

In a large heavy-bottomed pan, fry the onions and garlic in butter over a low heat until soft. Add the rice and stir until it is coated in the butter. Pour in the white wine and let it bubble up over the rice. Keep stirring and after a few minutes, add the squid ink, taking care not to let it spill. Now begin to add ladles of the stock, stirring continuously. This should take up to 25 minutes.

I have used uncooked prawns, rose petals, quantities of salt crystals and raw samphire for the image only.

To cook the prawns, toss in a pan of hot oil until opaque.

INGREDIENTS

Serves 4

- 300g risotto rice
- 800ml vegetable or fish stock
- 300ml white wine
- 2 cloves garlic
- Large knob of butter
- 20g squid ink
- Olive oil

KATAIFI PRAWNS

INGREDIENTS

Pull apart the strands of kataifi pastry and lay them on a clean surface. If not using immediately, keep the pastry covered with a damp tea towel to stop it drying out.

To cook, brush the pastry generously with melted butter. Dip the prawns into the sweet chilli sauce and push them gently on to the skewers, keeping them as straight as possible. Wrap the prawns lightly in the pastry and put to one side. In a deep pan, heat the oil to 160°C and carefully dip the skewers in. Cook each prawn stick for 3 minutes until golden brown. Then remove and place on some kitchen towel to soak up any excess oil.

Serve immediately with sweet chilli sauce or fresh mayonnaise.

Delicious!

- 10 fresh raw king prawns
- Thai sweet chilli sauce
- 10 skewers
- 180g kataifi pastry
- 125g butter, melted
- Vegetable oil for deep frying

THAI FISHCAKES

To make the pickle, heat the sugar and vinegar gently in a small saucepan until the sugar dissolves. Bring to the boil and let it bubble for 6-7 minutes until a thin syrup begins to form. Put to one side and leave to cool. Finely slice the carrot, cucumber, shallots and chilli and add to the cooled syrup, mixing thoroughly.

To make the fishcakes, crush the chillies, garlic, coriander, shallots, ginger, lime leaves and salt in a large mortar to form a paste. Mince the white fish in a food processor for a few seconds before placing into a mixing bowl and adding the spice paste. Combine the two thoroughly before adding the fish sauce and finely sliced green beans. Knead the mixture together firmly for a few minutes before dividing into balls.

Heat the oil in a large pan or deep fryer to 200°C and deep fry the fish for about 2-3 minutes until golden brown. Rest the fishcakes on kitchen towel to drain any excess oil before serving.

Sprinkle the crushed peanuts over the pickle and serve with the hot fishcakes.

Recipe adapted from *Vatch's Thai Street Food* by Vatcharin Bhumichtur.

INGREDIENTS

Serves 4

For the fish cakes:

4 small fresh red or green chillies (the latter for medium piquancy)

- 1 shallot, finely sliced
- 2 garlic cloves, peeled
- Handful of chopped coriander
- 1 tbsp finely chopped ginger
- 6 kaffir lime leaves, broken up
- 450g white fish fillet (cod, haddock, monkfish or any other white fish)
- 1 tbsp fish sauce
- Handful of very finely chopped green beans
- Salt to season
- Vegetable oil for deep frying

For the fish pickle:

- 125ml rice wine or white wine vinegar
- 2 tbsp granulated sugar
- 5cm piece of cucumber
- 1 small carrot
- 3 shallots finely sliced
- 1 medium fresh red chilli, finely sliced
- 1 tbsp crushed roasted peanuts

'to create a yearning'

SEAFOOD TAGLIATELLE

INGREDIENTS

Put some olive oil into a frying pan and fry off the bacon. After a few minutes, add the garlic, prawns and some lemon zest. If you like, you can add a splash of white wine at this stage, and allow to cook off.

Boil the pasta in a pan of salted boiling water and cook. In another pan, lightly boil the samphire in shallow water for two minutes. Drain both the pasta and the samphire and toss in a little olive oil and a handful of chopped parsley. Stir the prawn and bacon mix through the pasta and season with salt, pepper and a squeeze of fresh lemon.

Break the eggs into the pasta. Turn and serve immediately.

You could also add cream to the frying pan after adding white wine, to make a creamier, richer sauce.

Serves 4

- 400g fresh or dried pasta
- Samphire
- 1 clove garlic, chopped
- Olive oil
- 300g fresh peeled prawns
- Lemon, zest and juice
- 4 rashers of bacon, chopped (you can also use pancetta or lardons)
- Splash of white wine
- Handful chopped parsley
- 4 egg yolks

PISSALADIERE

INGREDIENTS

Serves 4

- 1 packet of puff pastry
- 3 tbsp olive oil
- Knob of butter
- 3 large onions
- 2 tbsp brown sugar
- 2 tbsp balsamic vinegar
- A pinch of provençal herbs
- Salt and pepper
- 100g anchovy fillets in olive oil
- About 12 pitted black olives.

Preheat the oven to 200°C. On a lightly floured surface, roll out the puff pastry to form a large rectangle approximately 0.5cm thick. In a frying pan, heat the olive oil and butter and cook the onions with the caramelising brown sugar and balsamic vinegar for around 40 minutes over a medium heat until soft.

Season with salt, pepper and a pinch of provençal herbs.

Spread the onion mix over the pastry, leaving an inch uncovered around the edges. Arrange the anchovies in a lattice style and stud-pattern the olives in between and bake in the oven for 25-30 minutes until the pastry is golden and the oil is sizzling.

Can be served warm or cold.

'the deep unnumbered waves of laughter of the sea'

Aeschylus

BEETROOT & LIQUORICE SOUP

Heat the coconut oil in a large pan and cook the onions until they begin to soften. Add the beetroot and ginger and cook for a few more minutes. Then add the stock cube to the boiling water and pour into the saucepan, before adding the liquorice and some ground pink peppercorns. Let the soup simmer on a low heat for 30-40 minutes or until the beetroot has fully softened.

Purée the soup and add the almond milk (or alternative). Sprinkle with chopped parsley and serve warm.

INGREDIENTS

Serves 4

- 1 tbsp virgin coconut oil
- 500g beetroot, peeled and cubed
- 1 large onion, diced
- 1 large knob of fresh ginger
- 2 tsp ground liquorice
- Pink peppercorns
- Salt to taste
- 1l boiling water
- Vegetable stock cube
- 125ml almond milk, soy milk or crème fraîche
- Handful of chopped parsley

The Tree

1980

how Do the man and woman meet before

the tree?

The wonder of manufacture – this,

the bird

knows for heaven: making as a gift

of flesh.

But making children live in air

Would redeem one Icarus whose eye is

Inward, twisted. He asks, absolute

why did the plant unfold in struggle,

seedling to seed to stalk to being?

He says, so absolute, I knew one

That in growing out grew in joy,

Master of a universe the locust plagued,

the land of a tree, a crying, laughing

Solitary who in the sky showered

And, down, entering in its root again,

Lovely and absurd and perverse,

each year rising disowning an old life,

Endlessly Cressid.

How Do the man and woman meet

before the tree, the special tree

of wood moving to flesh to mind almost

like Evil in operation through

wet mist after the air,

knocked by two or three live humans,

Salves itself again and sits and looks?

The man and woman meet.

Between their lips

As between each translation

the bare, uncultivatable stretch

holds motiveless communion.

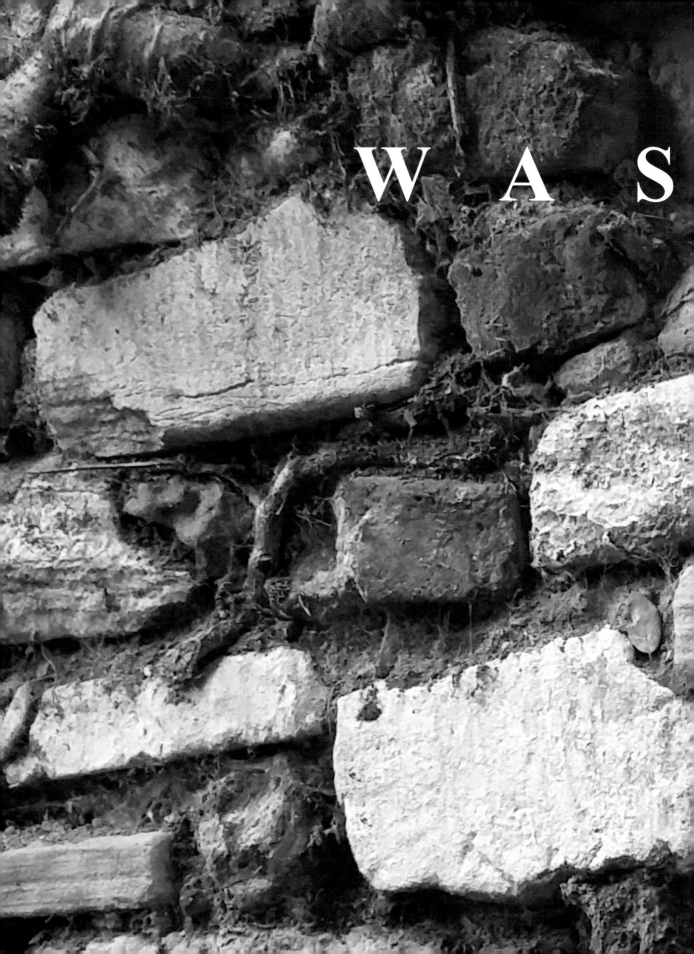

W A S

H E D

'to build the sky a vision'

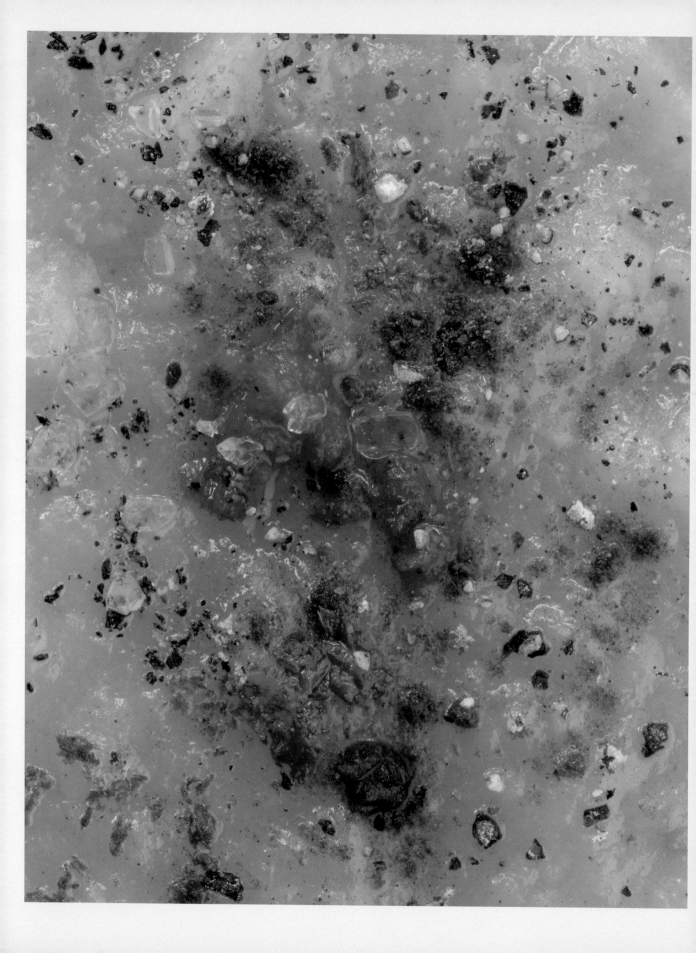

JERUSALEM ARTICHOKE SOUP

In a large soup pan, fry the onions in butter until softened. Add the Jerusalem artichokes and stock to the pot and bring to the boil. Then turn down the heat and gently simmer for at least 20 minutes until the vegetables are soft. Blend the mixture until completely smooth.

Garnish with sea salt, black pepper, spinach powder, cinnamon, porcini, parmesan, chives and double cream or crème fraiche. Serve.

INGREDIENTS

Serves 4

- Knob of butter
- 600g Jerusalem artichokes, scrubbed and sliced
- 600ml vegetable stock
- 1 large onion
- Sea salt
- Cracked black pepper
- Spinach powder
- Cinnamon
- Shredded porcini mushrooms
- Parmesan
- Chives
- Double cream or crème fraîche

TURKISH DELIGHT

Mix 1 tablespoon of rose water with 45ml cold water in a bowl. Lay the gelatine into the liquid and leave to soak.

Gently heat the sugar and 270ml water in a heavy based pan until the sugar has completely dissolved. Add the gelatine mixture to the pan stirring constantly until it has completely melted, then bring to the boil. Boil over a medium heat for 20 minutes, then remove from the heat and add the remaining rose water and the food colouring. Pour into a wetted tin and chill in the fridge for 24 hours until set.

Once set, sieve the icing sugar and cornflour over a sheet of baking parchment and turn the chilled Turkish delight out on to it. Cut into squares and toss in the sugar flour mixture, adding more icing sugar if necessary, until the squares are completely coated.

Store in greaseproof paper in an airtight container and sprinkle with more icing sugar before serving.

INGREDIENTS

- 2 tbsp rose water
- 25g gelatine
- 45ml cold water
- 270ml water
- 450g sugar
- A few drops of food colouring
- 25g icing sugar, plus extra
- 25g cornflour

'What is the Moon and what is it illuminating?'

'Slow deliberate delivery to let the savour sparkle. Respect your chosen grammar. Use the enjambment for what it is – a shift of the mind into another gear or image.'

BITTER CHOCOLATE LOAF

Heat the oven to 190°C and line a loaf tin with greaseproof paper.

Put the butter and chocolate into a saucepan and heat very gently until melted. Allow to cool for 5 minutes before whisking in the yogurt, eggs, coffee mixture and vanilla extract and add a pinch of salt. Mix the flour, cocoa powder, all the sugar and the bicarbonate of soda together and begin to add to the chocolate mix gradually. Once it forms a smooth batter, stir in the chocolate chips and pour into the loaf tin. If you feel the mixture is too runny, add a tablespoon of flour.

Bake for 45 minutes until a crack appears along the top of the cake. Test if it's ready by poking a skewer into the centre. It should come out clean. If the centre is still sticky leave in the oven for 5-10 more minutes. Remove from the oven and cool on a wire rack.

Serve warm with orange marmalade and crème fraîche, or chunks of honeycomb.

INGREDIENTS

- 200g self raising flour
- 50g cocoa powder
- 1/2 tsp bicarbonate of soda
- 175g unsalted butter
- Pinch of salt
- 100g caster sugar
- 75g dark muscovado sugar
- 100g natural greek yogurt
- 1 tsp vanilla extract
- 3 eggs
- 2tsp coffee granules, dissolved in 1 tbsp boiling water
- 100g dark chocolate (for melting)
- 75g dark chocolate chips

CURRIED OKRA WITH CHICKPEAS, TOMATOES AND BROCCOLI

Begin by trimming the stalks of the okra, keeping the tops intact and being careful not to cut into the pods. Heat a mixture of olive oil and vegetable oil in a pan and fry the onions and garlic until soft, stirring and adding the curry powder and the fresh chilli. Rinse the chickpeas and add to the pan along with the tinned tomatoes, cooking for 3 minutes. Finally add the okra, broccoli and fresh tomatoes and simmer, stirring occasionally, for 10 minutes until the okra is soft. Season with salt and pepper and serve.

INGREDIENTS

Serves 4

- 500g fresh okra
- 1 can of chickpeas
- 1 tin of chopped tomatoes
- Handful of cherry or baby plum tomatoes, chopped
- Half a head of broccoli, chopped
- 1 fresh red chilli, chopped
- 1 onion, chopped
- 2 cloves of garlic, chopped
- Olive oil
- Vegetable oil
- 2 tsp curry powder
- salt & pepper

RHUBARB AND PAN-FRIED TOMATO CRUMBLE

INGREDIENTS

Preheat the oven to 200°C. Melt the sugar and the butter in a pan. Chop the rhubarb and the tomatoes into chunks and add. Cook until softened.To make the crumble, cube the butter and begin to rub into the flour using your fingers until it starts to resemble breadcrumbs. Then add the sugar, a few generous pinches of poppy seeds and a pinch of salt and mix together.

Tip the crumble mixture over the rhubarb and tomato. Bake for 35-40 minutes until golden and bubbling and serve hot with single cream or custard.

Serves 4

For the filling:

- 400g rhubarb
- 75g caster sugar
- 3 or 4 plum tomatoes, halved

For the crumble:

- 50g caster sugar
- 150g plain flour
- 100g butter, plus extra for greasing
- Poppy seeds

'Food for the body, nourishment for the eyes, harmony and sounds for fullness of the heart.'

'And with the desire of a god I return
You to these rhythms of winter…'

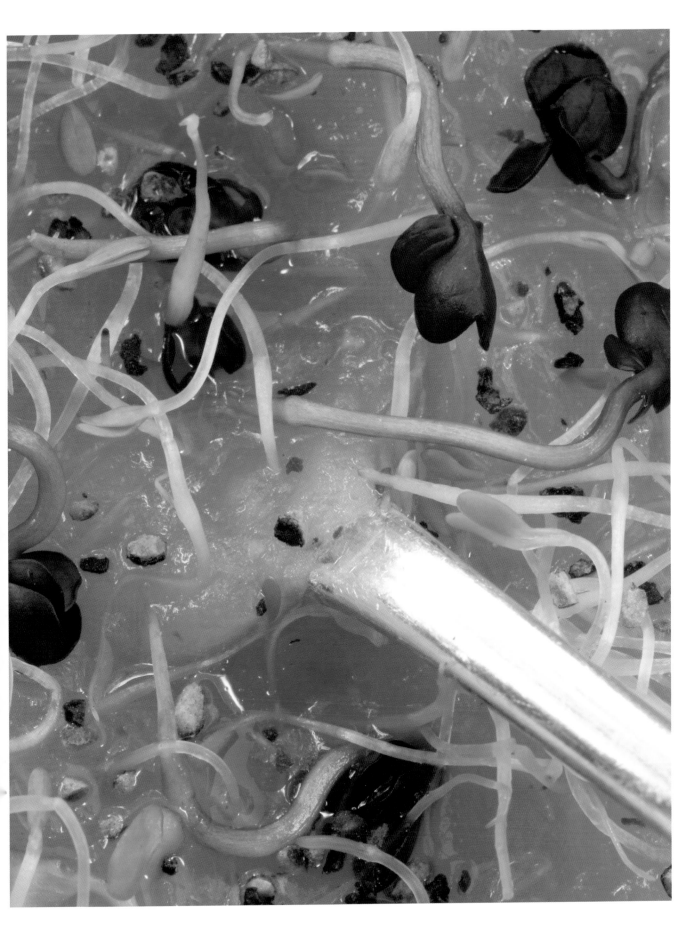

VENISON AND FRESH RASPBERRY STEW

Preheat the oven to 150°C. In a large casserole dish or heavy bottomed pan, fry the onions in olive oil and butter until golden. Add the garlic and the venison and brown the meat off. Once the meat is browned, add the wine, balsamic vinegar and stock and bring to the boil. Throw in the sliced carrots and the thyme, cover and place in the oven for at least an hour. 10 minutes before the end, add most of the punnet of raspberries to the casserole, stir well and place back in the oven for the remainder of the cooking time. Once removed from the oven, season to taste with salt and pepper.

To serve, stir through a generous handful of chopped parsley and scatter any remaining fresh raspberries on top.

INGREDIENTS

Serves 4

- 1 large onion
- 2 cloves garlic, crushed
- Olive oil
- Knob of butter
- 600g venison
- 1/3 bottle red wine
- 150ml beef stock
- A punnet of fresh raspberries
- 2 sprigs of thyme
- 2 tbsp balsamic vinegar (can also use raspberry vinaigrette)
- 2 carrots
- Handful of chopped parsley
- Knob of butter
- Salt and pepper

FRESH ONION SOUP (VEGAN)

Puree raw onions. Add the raw onions to a saucepan of diluted vegetable stock and heat.

To serve, sprinkle with quinoa and cracked black pepper.

INGREDIENTS

Serves 4

- 3 large white onions, diced
- 800ml vegetable stock
- Handful of sprouting quinoa
- Cracked black pepper

'and here we remain exploring…'

BAKED TROUT AND WILD RICE

Preheat the oven to 210°C. Lay the trout on a sheet of aluminium foil. Slice and place lemons inside. Season and wrap the fish. Put into the oven for 15-20 minutes, depending on the size.

Cook and drain wild rice and serve the baked trout on top.

INGREDIENTS

Serves 4

- A large whole fresh trout
- 2 lemons, sliced
- 220g wild rice

B A

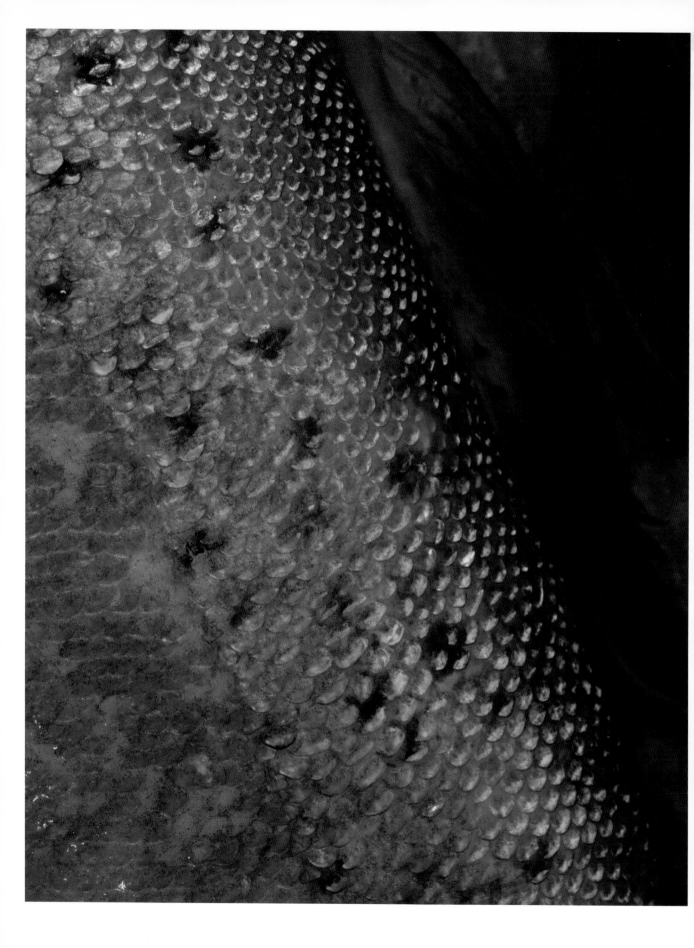

'Picnic under a Wellingtonia…'

FAVA BEAN SOUP

In a large saucepan, soften the onions in butter and a little olive oil. Add the chicken stock and bring to the boil. Add the fava beans and a little salt and pepper and leave to simmer for 20 minutes or until the beans have softened. Blend the soup until smooth.

To serve, sprinkle with chilli flakes or a handful of grated parmesan and enjoy with flatbread or crackers.

INGREDIENTS

Serves 4

- 1 large onion
- Olive oil
- Knob of butter
- 600ml chicken stock
- 500g fresh fava beans (broad beans), peeled
- Salt and pepper

GOAT CURRY

For a creamier consistency halve the amount of beef stock and add half a can of coconut milk.

Place the onion, garlic and ginger in a food processor and blend until they form a paste. In a heavy-bottomed pan, heat the oil and cook the onion mixture for a few minutes. Add the chopped chilli, curry powder, a small bunch of curry leaves and the thyme sprigs and cook for a further few minutes. Dice the goat shoulder into small pieces and add to the pan, browning off the meat. Once browned, add the tinned tomatoes and stock and bring to the boil, cooking for 10 minutes. Then reduce the heat to a simmer, cover and leave to cook slowly for 2 1/2 to 3 hours. Remove the lid for the final 30 minutes of cooking before adding the drained can of beans to heat through. Add a generous squeeze of lemon juice and a handful of chopped coriander.

Serve immediately with a handful of rocket and warm flatbread to accompany.

INGREDIENTS

- 1 large onion
- 8-10 cloves of garlic
- 100g chopped ginger
- 100 ml vegetable oil
- 1 scotch bonnet
- Curry leaves
- 3 sprigs of thyme
- 700g goat shoulder
- 4 tbsp curry powder
- 1 can (400g) tinned tomatoes
- 1 can (400g) kidney beans
- 300ml beef stock
- Lemon juice
- Handful of chopped coriander
- Handful of rocket (to serve)
- Flatbread (to serve)

'The lotion of the forest is the walk to the rebel children here among the reaching plants our balm is our loss and the return of the inevitable reconciliation. This is why the synonymity of death with birth is the only cliché (it is inevitable, and irony is pain) – we can create our loss because we can create our discovery.'

'Remember the aim is to nourish the spirit
and the work will follow…'

CHESTNUT SOUP

'Place the chestnuts, onion, celery, stock and the bay leaf into a large saucepan and heat until boiling. Turn down the heat, cover and simmer for 45 minutes. Blend the soup until smooth, seasoning with salt and pepper to taste and, if you like, add a dash of double cream. Serve with a little sprinkled nutmeg'.

INGREDIENTS

Serves 4

- 200g whole chestnuts, cooked and peeled
- 1 onion, diced
- 1 large stick of celery, chopped
- 1 litre of ham or vegetable stock
- 1 bay leaf
- Double cream
- Salt and pepper
- Nutmeg

'The artist must be prince; his lieutenant keeps
the throne spick and span'

SPICED STEWED APPLES WITH SAGE

INGREDIENTS

Peel the apples and cut into cubes. Place in a saucepan over a low heat with a splash of cold water, a generous squeeze of lemon juice and the sugar. Let this begin to heat for a few minutes before adding the cloves, cinnamon and prunes. Continue to simmer on a low heat for 15 minutes until the apples completely soften but do not disintegrate, adding a few torn sage leaves towards the end. The softer you want your apples to be, the longer the cooking time.

Serve warm or cold with cream, yogurt or crème fraiche.

- 2 large Bramley apples
- Lemon juice
- 8 pitted prunes
- 6 cloves
- Small handful of sage leaves
- 2 tbsp caster sugar
- 1/4 tsp cinnamon

CARAMELISED ORANGES

INGREDIENTS

- 5 oranges
- 100g sugar
- 6 tbsp water

Zest and juice one of the oranges and place to one side. With the remaining four, peel the outer skin and slice across the centre to form wheel shaped segments about 1cm thick.

In a pan begin to melt the sugar and water over a medium heat until it forms a caramel. Let it simmer, without stirring, for a few minutes until bubbling. One by one add the orange segments to the pan, coating each side with the caramel, and removing after a few minutes. Once all the oranges have been caramelised, add the orange juice and zest to the remaining caramel to form a sauce and then pour over the oranges.

COCONUT ALMOND BALLS

In a pan heat the oil to 160°C. In a bowl mix together the almonds, coconut, sugar, icing sugar, eggs, flour and lemon juice to form a runny paste. Add the flour bit by bit to thicken the mixture until it becomes a sticky dough. Roll the mixture into balls and coat in flaked almonds. Carefully place the balls into the hot oil and deep fry for 5 minutes until each one is golden brown and crispy. Let them drain on kitchen paper to soak up any excess oil, and serve hot drizzled in maple syrup.

INGREDIENTS

- 200g desiccated coconut
- 200g ground almonds
- 150g icing sugar
- 150g caster sugar
- 1 tbsp lemon juice
- 2 eggs
- 50g plain flour (use more if mixture needs thickening)
- Flaked almonds
- Vegetable oil for deep frying
- Maple syrup (to serve)

'love is children talking in air'

'love is children walking in air'

'and you, warm ocean, are my daughter'

PARSNIP & VIOLET PAVLOVA

Preheat the oven to 150°C. Place the egg whites into a clean bowl and whisk at medium speed until they form stiff peaks. Gradually add the sugar and continue to whisk. Once all the sugar is added, whisk at a higher speed for 5 minutes until the meringue becomes glossy, being careful not to let the mixture collapse.

Line a baking tray with baking parchment and spread the mixture into a rough circle, creating a nest shape. Bake the meringue for 1 hour until it becomes very lightly coloured. Turn off the oven but leave the meringue in for another hour as the oven cools. This should stop the meringue from collapsing whilst ensuring it remains soft inside

Peel and grate the parsnips in a bowl, add the lemon juice, zest and the icing sugar and mix together to form the filling. Whip the double cream and begin to fill the cooled pavlova with the cream and the parsnip mixture. Decorate with crystallised violets and miniature meringue kisses.

INGREDIENTS

To Samuel Beckett

Serves 8

For the meringue:

- 4 egg whites
- 225g caster sugar

For the filling:

- 3 large parsnips, grated
- 1 large lemon, zested and juiced
- 100g icing sugar
- 200ml double cream
- Handful of crystallised violets
- Miniature meringue kisses

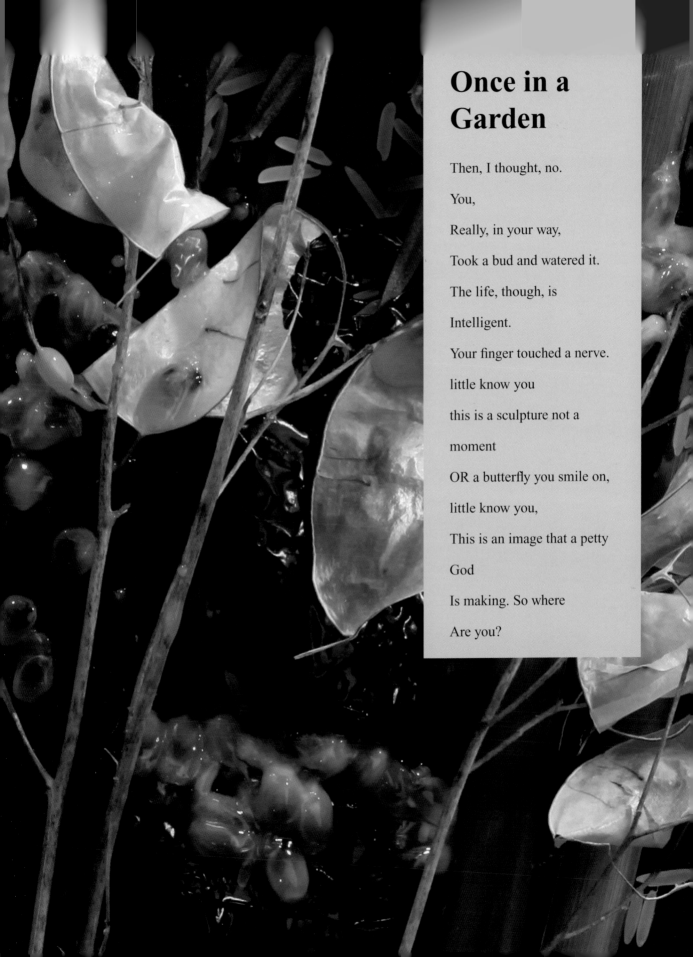

Once in a Garden

Then, I thought, no.

You,

Really, in your way,

Took a bud and watered it.

The life, though, is

Intelligent.

Your finger touched a nerve.

little know you

this is a sculpture not a

moment

OR a butterfly you smile on,

little know you,

This is an image that a petty

God

Is making. So where

Are you?

Untitled

1978

nothing withers in white Narcissi,

clean and cut

like sweet juice on grass stalks.

They just, well,

Grow and are admired for their

Vast determination,

Always thinking that everything matters

Inside the curve

Of the beautiful smell the smooth face

Emanates, unconsciously,

Of course, what else, what else, no

One small blames them.

Crocus

Each stem beautiful

And shaking. Yellow

Petals closed, rise out

From green beds. In sun fall

Entire, special, profane

O My young girl, these

Flowers are mothers.

'the {poetry} wood where Narcissus lives is
filling slowly with things. Right in the centre,
I see a flowered tomb.'

BAKLAVA

'To make the syrup; dissolve the sugar in the water and bring to the boil. Let it boil for for 5-6 minutes until it has thickened. Then add the rose water, lemon juice and pieces of orange zest (for flavour) and simmer gently for a few more minutes. Remove the orange zest and leave to cool. It is important that the syrup is fully cooled before pouring it over the pastry as hot syrup will soften the pastry layers

Heat the oven to 180°C. Blitz the nuts together in a food processor and then mix through the ground cinnamon and ground cloves. Grease an oven tray, with sides at least 5cm high, with some of the melted butter and begin to lay out the filo pastry. To stop the pastry from drying out, cover it with a damp tea towel whilst working. Gently layer sheets of filo pastry in the tin brushing each layer with melted butter. After 4 layers spread over half the nut mixture, repeat with another 4 layers of filo, and then the rest of the nut mixture. Top with the final 4 layers of filo and brush generously with the remaining butter.

Partially cut the baklava into squares or diamonds and bake in the oven for 30 minutes until they turn a pale golden colour. Increase the temperature to 220°C and bake for a further 10-15 minutes until crisp. Remove from the oven and pour over half the syrup mixture. Allow to cool for 5 minutes before pouring over the rest of the mixture. Remove from the tray using a palette knife and sprinkle with the remaining chopped pistachios.

Baklava can be stored in the refrigerator for 3-4 days after baking.

INGREDIENTS

- 100g walnuts
- 100g almonds
- 100g pistachios, plus an extra handful to sprinkle over the top
- 2tsp ground cinnamon
- 1/2tsp ground cloves
- 200g butter, melted
- 2 × 270g packets (12 sheets) of filo pastry

For the syrup:
- 500g sugar
- 275ml water
- 1/2 tsp lemon juice
- 1-5 tbsp rose water (depending on taste)
- 2 large pieces of orange zest

SEARED TUNA WITH KIWI FRUIT AND BUTTERED LEEKS

INGREDIENTS

Rub each tuna steak with a little olive oil and set aside to rest. Chop the leeks diagonally into segments. Put the butter in a pan over a medium heat and add the leeks, turning them to coat them fully in the butter. Then lower the heat, cover the pan and cook gently for 15 minutes. In the meantime prepare the kiwi by skinning and slicing into discs. Heat a griddle pan and once it's hot carefully place the steaks onto the griddle. Cook each side for two minutes, a little longer if the steaks are quite thick. Meaty fish is best served a little pink in the middle. Season with salt and pepper and serve with the hot buttered leeks and a few slices of the kiwi, squeezing a little lemon juice over the whole dish.

Garnish with sashimi ginger.

Serves 4

- 4 tuna steaks
- Olive oil
- 4 leeks
- 50g butter
- Salt and pepper
- 2 kiwi fruit
- Lemon juice
- Sashimi ginger

HONEY ROAST HAM WITH SPICED FRUIT AND CAPERS

INGREDIENTS

Place the gammon in a very large saucepan and cover with cold water. Bring to the boil and cook according to its weight – approximately 20 minutes per 500g. Once cooked, drain and cut away the skin from the ham, leaving a layer of fat behind. Lightly score in a criss-cross pattern and stud with cloves. Preheat the oven to 170°C.

To make the glaze, put all the ingredients into a pan over a low heat and simmer until you have a glossy syrup. Put half the syrup over the meat and roast for 15 minutes. Pour on most of the rest of the glaze, leaving a little aside for the fruit, and return to the oven for 35 minutes until golden brown, basting with the juices frequently.

Chop the fruits, and mix with the star anise and any remaining glaze, and squeeze some fresh orange juice over the top. Season with salt and pepper and serve with diced onion and capers. Ham, a versatile meat, is delicious warm or cold.

1 large unsmoked boneless gammon joint

Handful of cloves

For the glaze:
- 200g dark brown sugar
- 200ml runny honey
- 2 tbsp dijon mustard
- Handful of kumquats
- Handful of star anise (no more than 5)
- 2 kiwi fruit
- 12-15 medjool dates
- Juice of 1 orange
- 1 onion, finely chopped
- A jar of capers

PAPAYA SALAD

Place the garlic and chillies in a large mortar and crush.

Add the beans, tomato and papaya and beat together very lightly.

Then add the fish sauce, sugar and lime juice, stirring well before seasoning with salt and pepper. Serve with shredded iceberg lettuce etc.

Recipe adapted from 'Vatch's Thai Street Food' by Vatcharin Bhumichtur

INGREDIENTS

This spicy fruit salad (som tam) is an extremely popular north-eastern Thai dish.

Serves 2

- 2 garlic cloves, peeled
- 3-4 small fresh red or green chillies
- Handful of green beans, chopped
- 1 large tomato, or a handful of cherry tomatoes
- 175g fresh papaya, peeled, de-seeded and cut into segments
- 2 tbsp fish sauce
- 1 tbsp granulated sugar
- 2 tbsp lime juice
- Salt and pepper to season
- Iceberg lettuce to serve

'what is the water? It is the thought and the life'

July 1998

The air is hot and the road

Fresh with a day of rain

And I cannot think of anything

But the future and what it holds

So that the smell of the cleansed

Road, metallic in its sure erotic

Invisibility and aura, beds my

Mind, takes it from its ceilings

Of raw innocences, the catholic altars

In the mountain range all about

And Returns it to the calm corrupting scent

Of the World going on, going on, going on

'how do I get

from the poems
into the eye?'

Levée

'Language rescues something.
I don't know what...'

'There's no perception without love'

His Job is Love:
'poetry expiates'

'to be without breath'
Breathlessness

'but the inhering spirit is light and
cool and is the arrow pointing to
a new beginning…'

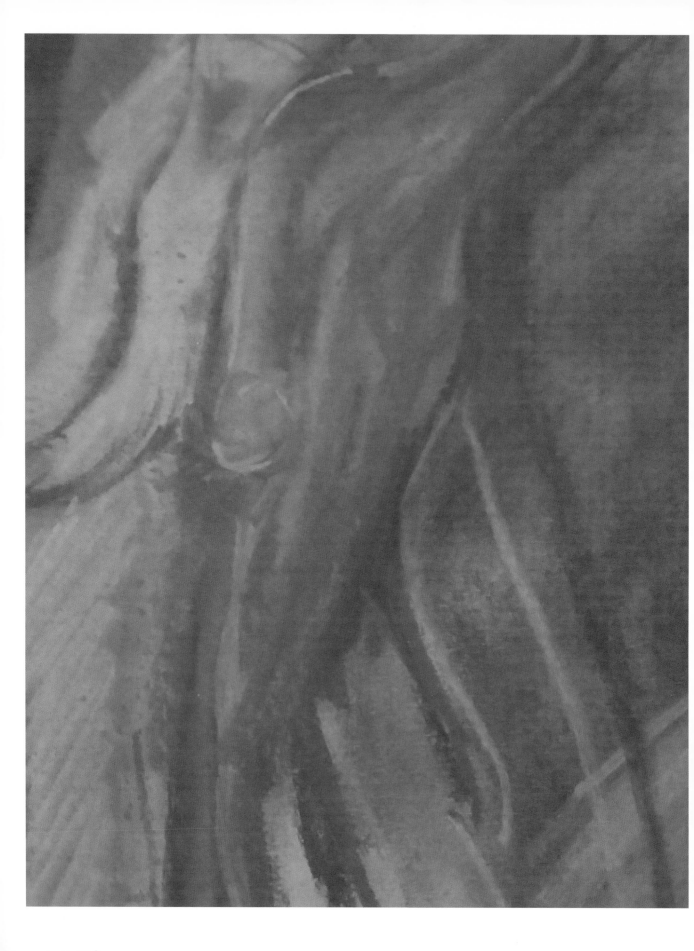

'For is this grace, this is happen'

'so what you might do, gives colour'

GUY BARKER

BORN 27 JANUARY ...

In the end
we are ourselves
in the world torment
Nor the cruelty ...
...

The washing of the feet

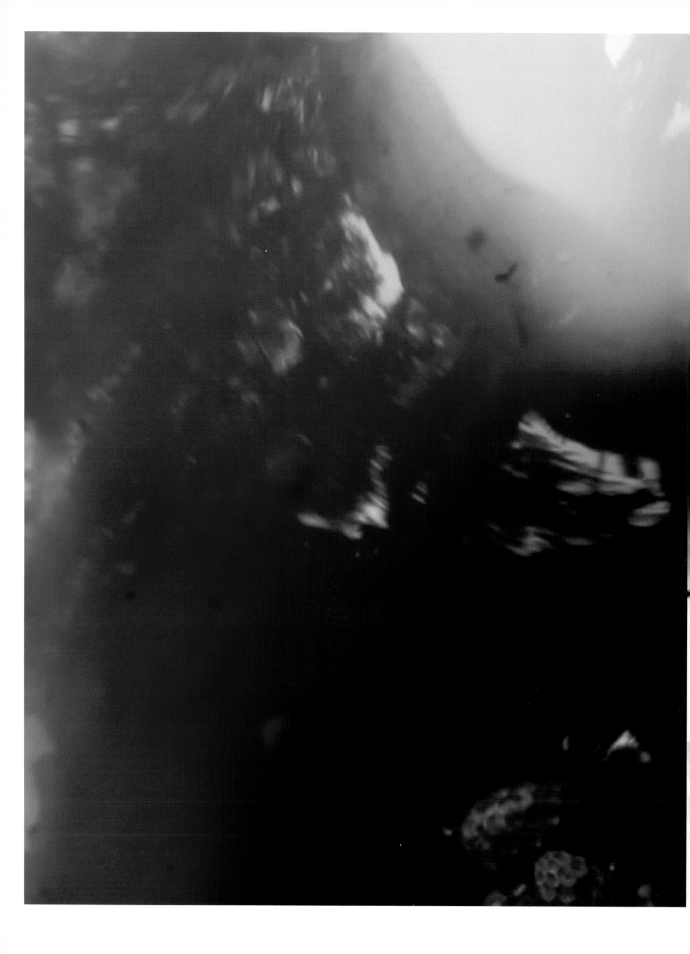

'the cave washing the water'

'so it is fitting the warm hands are with the mind'

'Sound is only sound

where there is an ear'

'When you are full of green wine
Think of me in the ash of the powdered soil
Your tale limbs walking the far walk
And you can lift your glass clear'

'the ritual of the dying god releasing new energies'

NOTES

'leaves fall but they never laugh loud,
only words last.'

In memory of Guy
1960-2009

Tenants of the House

1979

How time does move quietly over the lapping

Benches of this city lapping like water

Against the broken breaking word.

What noise does the tree make? I have forgotten

Telling nothing. We tell nothing, hung in wind.

The air is stilled as ice yet flows feinting

Like the shot whale, a hundred cells falling.

There is not time enough to watch the living

Only time to sleep within its eye. Destroy

The hour, destroy this planetary dream

And let us doze, my love, upon the rain.

Father O Father, bless your bright infant

Who walks toward the turning wall,

Pray the sin within out blood might spill

Painting the inconclusive idea over the tired air

Let bell announce the bird song to our slovenly ear.

Why wait, my love, till spring, why wait within

The skull of king and martyr,

Why wait where the empty answer whispers

In the movement of paper on pavement

Over the benches of this city lapping like water

Against the broken word of desolated mind.

Even shadowed be, and the dome of your brow,

Asleep as a night bird, might call me back

To hearing the sun belt out is promises. Quiet,

For it is outside our dark cave that desire lies.

After fire upon the flesh and on the bone

Our eye that hunts its mind's cell falls over,

No longer foraging at the gate of the mind's cell.

Our mouth is saying the speech of a million,

Cutting off the pieces for the fine work,

Preparing the flesh for a whiter death.

And that we can live as the dead do,

Is it our purpose.

Court Green, North Tawton, Devon EX20 2EX
5 March 98

Dear John Venning —

3 years ago you sent me poems by Guy Barker — in a very pretty cover of stiff canvas.

Catching up on my mail I discovered these, and just read them.

I was mightily struck by the bite and intelligence — the verve

and musical control. Something
extremely interesting there, without
any doubt.

I wonder what's happened to
him since.

Yours

Ted Hughes

Credences

1982

I

These doves with clipped wings, their mothers arguing

On foreign branches, are as ignorant

Ambassadors, more delicate with the air

Than any grand official on the quai d'orsay.

They fly whitening through the uncarved darknesses

Of summer, through this crazed window, raising

An untheatrical hell. It is not that they fear me.

I fear them for they do not love me

Nor the ungracious eyes that greedily

Bite at their grace. The adamantine

Mind, with its desire, clasps our love

To our hate, and with generosities

Touches the body of your midnight song,

Fruiting alone without the virginal of doves

The fat and unenviable falsities.

My house is the same in the winter

For my brain's body loves her own love

While mist sits on the edge of sleep

II

Your hand in the green water clears away

The predictions of this strong river,

Makes the choir in my eyes

Quiet, not in reverence, but abashed

At the thin elegance of your pizzicato.

Love is the home of the brilliant soul,

Unstifled by the death of our season.

Summer breathes motioning in its

Direction to unstable the locked brain,

Stale in its selfishness, resting on fictions.

As my syllables run, they laugh, they die

So evenings die, on the clear viol of memory.

Theodora

1993

How you are in the hours of your kisses,

Turning your hair over and over and always

Infecting love, or pleasure, with Joy. You hold

Honey in my eyes, though I see no hand

Pointing it there, nor smell; yet, and yet,

You do not know the passing away of all

Of this: death is not in your joy, but yes

In mine, talking it down in the reddening hours.

II

When you again, in the white light, curl

Up and lozenges of fear go away in a scatter,

The trumpets shout up the dust, armoured

Knights linger bragging their unlinked chains,

When you, excusing yourself for lack of ready

Centimes, angel-tread on the cinders askance;

O the weak guarantees of desire, see them croak

Through the typhoon, hysterical green rain girl,

Wettening your wallet, blotting the ink-dreams

Of the liberal world: I speak then, you listen to the air.

III

I am the poet and the signifier and you, warm

Ocean, are my daughter. Let me now think

You my soul, without its betrayals, there fine

In its pale-blue youth, nor let me take you into

Design for a fresher world. You, my dear love

Are born for pain, though the air will cool your scars

And the cicatrices will rest after the violet

Rage. He spare you, the so beautiful?

No, for look, as I drink, salt bites my lips.

IV

Collapsing sometime, like an ancient bridge, am I

Halting the flow-chart of our evil negatives,

Platforming and dicing-out my favourite Quixotes

Or do I speak the real big Game, without

Me, and the residues of wine. May I climb

Indomitable, making ash holly and oak Judas,

May I love you truly as you see me

Daubed in integrity, driving my angelic tyres

With the wish my smile would not know.

If I could sniff glue the solvent would burn you,

Lord, and the black wasting paper would find

The puzzles gone and the Turtle and I alone.

Excerpt from a postcard, 5th July, 2003

LE ROYAUME DU SILENCE

5/7/03

DEAR INIGO,

I HAVE NEVER HAD THE COURAGE NOR FITNESS TO DO
THIS BUT THE DESCRIPTION IS TRUE - YOU SOMETIMES
FEEL THIS IS AN AEROPLANE LOOKING OUT OVER THE
CLOUDS BUT IMAGINE WALKING ON THE CRISP SNOW
ABOVE THE CLOUDS AND WITH THE SUN AROUND YOU
LIKE A BROTHER OR SISTER!

LOTS OF LOVE FROM DADDY X

Consuelo

April 1989

1.

How would I say you then

In my uncertain love but to turn you

Through heavens

Awarding you this name

And that, unprotected from the assent

Of your soul.

2.

O your eyes, true enough

Almost walk into mine as summer air

To open doors

And your rare brown hair

Puts out my mind, winding its pathway

To this stair.

3.

Lost and yet not quite

For I did hear you speak in so many

Silences to me

And who I hear just now

Is the great wasted land itself

Flowering water.

4.

We would sit on the rocks,

By angels, entranced in the rhythming

Lamb

And they would apron us

Within His golden blue, the white bright radiant

Blood.

5.

How would we not serve Him

Breaking the wounds with pale Longinus'

Gift,

How would we speak back

Into speech, light love in a fire

Lisping.

6.

We would be in His cup

Yea, laid down in the green meadow-sweet

Perfectly fooled.

Consuelo and Inigo

1996

She dances over

the simpler sun

over the burning

sun she dances

step by step the

method breaks up

in a forgetful

summer she dances

cooling the lashes

of her boy the

burning sun she

dances and all

death is light

as the trill

she danced that day

to the dead air.

2.

There that he were

preceding the sadnesses

over the cold danceless

grass is slight

dew pinching only

his soul his breath

fast in the red breeze

and she always she

kicking at the syntax

mother courage

mother courage you

cannot break up

the stars the stars

and their hardnesses

were he that there.

3.

In his irises she slept

sleeping of dream laughter

with the brave shield

aluminium brave in his

eyes this boy a warrior

of visitation to her river

bank his mother

of sleep curling her

emerald stem about

slim fingers twisting

the hidden interlude

of all the burnt day

the black mezzos in the

centre of the moon slept she

in his irises slept she.

'that the whole of life is the SOUL
remembering the PAST. (The present
passing.) Somehow the soul is watching
as it were a scene passing away before
its EYES.'

INIGO, MY SON

He is the sun remembered in the white hay

In the drunken noon of mid July

When my eyes are blinded by the high light

And my mind is whirring in a happy sleep.

He is blue eyed like the sea, blond like the moon.

He is meek and he is cruel; he wields each baton

Ike a sword and every plate is his shield.

Waking the Family

2000. Translated into Chinese for 'Our Common Sufferings: An Anthology of World Poets in Memoriam 2008 Sichuan Earthquake'.

I have the wheat, the half-open flowers,

The forget-me-nots, buttercups, exquisite roses,

I have the bloom of the lily-of-the-valley,

I have its fragrance.

Saint Therese of Lisieux

When my eyes are closed and in the confusion of

All the light inside my skull,

I am writing on a remembrance, like an item on a list

Of exemplary "To Do's" of the person

Or group that I am meant still to meet; they are a sacred family

Touting for a lift from a passing bus, they squint at my

Puzzlement in an ineffable silence, moving in their

Perfectly coloured clothes as if about to begin

The important journey, not a final curtain call,

But the beginning of a major passage through mountains

They will never own or know, a family of marmosets

With a mission beyond the forest's warm cover. They

Are always ready, gathering their belongings

Shifting back their out-of-place locks from their white eyes

That are cast in different directions, looking as if one, like the

Burghers of Calais, grouped together yet quietly in

Despair moving up through the flattening mist.

Who are these lovers of mine, my closest destinies, lilacs

Of the soul, waiting upon my disappearing self?

I know I am required to meet them, pass my hand to

Them like a Visa to a border guard, wait with them

As they make their chartings of the mountains,

Remembering in advance the past that becomes now and

The future that is heady longing, remembering the wind

That has breathed by over me into the watery reeds, warming

The early steps around the mountain plains.

My mind is the summit of this mountain, the central one

In the perfectly immobile range that cannot smile

Nor speak nor show anger, remaining always either

The beneficent friend or the indifferent enemy.

I do not know where I am but beneath my feet

Is silver grass, remnants of a moon-spangled banner

And fields and fields of question marks begging

For attention. Am I in heaven here? Or

In a mirror of mirrors, holding

A final picture of green and blue wild as honey water?

The group of shuffling persons is near again,

Angling across the skyline, a jagged shadowed group

Of Desperate intimacy, looking through blind eyes as the day goes.

The border guards are gone, my visa is damp and blurred,

A memory of the future, coveting a history of eclipses

In an undertone, in the silence of a few pages,

A visa stamped for one visit. Do I search for the family

Or are they searching for me? Why are they blind

On the mountain summit yet walk with a deliberation,

A likelihood of getting somewhere, through the storm garden,

Purposeful against my unpurpose, my inevitability?

I wish them to be the future held up

In a cup of warm hands, the garland of barbaric smiles.

汉英双语版 Chinese - English

让我们共同面对灾难

世界诗人同祭四川大地震

Our Common Sufferings:

An Anthology of World Poets in Memoriam
2008 Sichuan Earthquake

聂珍钊 罗良功 编

Edited by Nie Zhenzhao & Luo Lianggong

上海外语教育出版社
SHANGHAI FOREIGN LANGUAGE EDUCATION PRESS

唤醒家人

——献给在四川大地震中受难的人们

盖伊·巴克（英国）

我拥有小麦，半合半开的花，

勿忘我、毛茛花、雅洁的玫瑰花，

我拥有绽放的铃兰百合，

我拥有花朵的芳香。

——圣女小德兰

当我的眼睛闭上，辨不清

头颅内奕然生光的一切，

我期待着被记起，就像那个

或者那群我打算见面的人

通常列出的要做事情的清单

中的一个事项。他们是一个神圣的家庭

招呼过路的巴士顺带他们一程，在难以言说的沉默中

斜眼瞅瞅我的困惑，摆动他们

色彩斑斓的衣服，仿佛即将开始

那次重要的旅行，不是最后的谢幕，

而是一段穿越群山的主要行程的开始。

这个绢猴家族，永远不会拥有或者知晓这群山，却

负着超越温暖的森林华盖的使命。他们

时刻做好了准备，收拾起自己的物品，

把遮住眼睛的蓬乱的毛发卷披到脑后，他们的白眼
投向不同的方向。看起来这个家庭，就像
法国加来港的居民一样静静地聚集在一起，
在越来越薄的雾气中绝望地向上攀行。
我的这些亲爱的人是谁，这些最亲近我的、
等待着我正在消失的自我的命运之神，
这些从灵魂开出的紫丁香？
我知道我要去会见他们，向他们伸出
我的手，就像向边防卫兵递上签证。当他们
在绘制山地路线图时与他们一起等待，并提前
回忆起已成为现在的过去和
仍然只是令人陶醉的渴望的将来，回忆那风——
风掠过我进入水泽里的芦苇中，温暖着
山区平坝上早起的脚步。

我的心是这座山的顶峰，位于山脉的
中段，这山脉完全静止，不会微笑
不会说话不会表现愤怒，始终是
仁慈的朋友或者冷漠的敌人。
我不知道我在哪儿，在我脚下
是银色的草，月光装点的旗帜的碎片
和大片大片祈求关注的
问号。我已在天堂了吗？或者
只是在万镜之镜中捕捉到了
最后的碧青湛蓝的图景、柔和的如甜蜜的水波？
那个混乱的人群又走近了，

望天际，分明是一个彼此紧紧依偎
差不齐的剪影，在流逝的日子里用失明的眼睛在张望。
蹒跚而行的人群再次临近。
防卫兵已经离去，我的签证潮湿了模糊了。
声的纸页里有着对未来的记忆，潜藏着
消失历史的觊觎。
证，盖着一次往返的印章。我要寻找我的家人
者，他们正在寻找我吗？他们在高山之巅
眼睛为什么看不见脚步却又那样沉着，
仿佛他们穿过这暴风雨的花园一定会走到什么地方？
他们走向目标的脚步与我的无目标、我的必然相反。
我希望他们成为握在一起的温暖的手
擎起的未来，希望他们是那最质朴的微笑
组成的花环。

（Trans. Li Haiming & Luo Lianggong 李海明 罗良功 译）

ISBN 978-7-5446-1064-3

9 787544 610643 >

定价：38.00 元

'And then, do we give up? We can't.'

Untitled.

2/8/90

from Woodyates Manor.

Waiting again for the lively

Point of desire, the walk out from Zion,

Tied to a black leopard

Waiting again

The uncharming concentration

Burnt at the fire gate

Waiting again for the repeating

Propulsion, the hero without helmet,

This time, wax-drops spat

Upon his fore-arms - holiday memories -

His hair long like a wand

Waiting again

And waiting again, quite over-glut

With distances, alarms and choices.

'I must, Lord, make my contract; riding up the bough and swinging down on it, I the boy must force the green to its heaven. Oh you are the most loveable of all,

. . . . S . . . . . . P . . . . . . R . . . . . I . . . . . N . . . . . . T . . . . . . I . . . . . N . . . . . . G . . .

through the wind, you in every pretty thing, my sleep, the eyes and joy of my son, the deep laughter of Theodora, her distance from nothing, it is all yours, you stunt the fire stones and everything that is yours is by sufferance. How can we be within words after your crazy face, having loved it so with its excitements. I say this on the edge of death, always seeking the end of time of time.'

Ombra Mai Fu

1982

Of Credere

O there is no other ever

in this hour of our fortune

though it seem so now like a dark car

throughout these fine urbanities

the dawn wind our covenant

with oiled wing and unsung messages

O no other is there ever

though it seem so now

in this new year of our fortune

perfecting the van of our survivals

that it may drive the angel Gabriel

upon white tarmac in the western lands

O we never do sell our love

at the edge of the motorway wall

where the sun drains out the nations

in among the rolling stones

under the drill of myriad engines

and the faint speeches fighting

O once upon a time

in the blue of your rhyme, the red of your blood

you looked so fine

tested at Meriba and in the desert at Massa

2. Of Him

In the ever He falls, where we are,

draymen of love heaving out His

barrels, one two, one two, for so long

burning in the flame in the palace arena

of Nebuchadnezzar, eyes inward

with the coldsmooth hand of a fourth

(in light) against our almost disbelieving
temples that bloodflow like huge calmed
oceans, sleeping the dolphins therein,
the wild killers thereunder, forever and
for ever and ever amen, so amor vincit
in the ever, mysterium fidei, amen amen.

3. Of Her

The blades wipe and the emerald hill appears,
son fils est venu, during the very longest
summer morning when Her warm breath
would not leave off, she claimed our palms
where the dimes unfurled for the cost
of a local paper (Bless the world). Every
pedestrian tremble has hidden under Her,
through all voices, the high arches cancelling
death (and taxes), all the bright scars
pitching and breaking the good early days,
the solstice morning is underneath Her,
graced blue in the penitentiary of england.
So the blades wipe, the donkey spills the apple
Through the television screen and the tender land.

4. Laus tibi, christe

Father of hosts, spirit whose bare feet march
over akeldama, soaked pink in the oblique dew,
you, whose eyes smell meek-scented lovers
when they sleep not there but under
the golden of our ministers, O most lovable
space, generous your nature though softly
betrayed after every renewal, we weep too
in this petty field, mistaking the deep lights
on the blooded grass for your love's pennies
spilling to save, the air light now in showers
and all roses new flesh over the terrified land.

THANK YOU

You were different.

Unusual.

And you are deeply missed.

'how do the man and woman meet?'

Wedding Song

1978

At the side of the river

I made you memorable,

I made you

Where the water is

And how it wakes me

When it breaks its sheets

On the river walls.

How the water does these things

Is you. Your tepid fingers

Touched and I sang.